ALLEN CARR'S
NO MORE
HANGOVERS

ALLEN CARR'S
NO MORE
HANGOVERS

Alcohol: the Easyway solution

ARCTURUS

Arcturus Publishing Limited
26/27 Bickels Yard
151–153 Bermondsey Street
London SE1 3HA

Published in association with
foulsham
W. Foulsham & Co. Ltd,
The Publishing House, Bennetts Close, Cippenham,
Slough, Berkshire SL1 5AP, England

ISBN 0-572-03073-8

This edition printed in 2005

British Library Cataloguing-in-Publication Data: a catalogue record for this
book is available from the British Library

Printed in England

Dedication

It gives me great pleasure to dedicate this book to Crispin Hay.

Cris is not only a close friend and colleague, but also Easyway's leading pathfinder in helping others escape the tyranny of the bottle.

Without his commitment, expertise and compassion, this book would not have been possible.

INTRODUCTION

In 1983 I discovered something every smoker dreams of – an easy way to stop smoking. I quit my previous career and set out to cure the world of smoking. I am now widely regarded as the world's leading expert on helping smokers quit. My book *The Easy Way to Stop Smoking* has sold over five million copies, and my network of clinics spans the globe.

But my success has not been limited to smokers. I have helped people with a variety of problems, from overeating to substance addiction to fear of flying.

The irony is that for many years I was consuming more and more of the most widely available 'substance' of all.

I found a solution to my predicament, and I am delighted to share it with you.

ALCOHOL IS EVERYWHERE

It is consumed by 90 per cent of UK adults. But few stop to question their assumptions about booze. The media don't help when they bandy about misleading phrases such as 'alcohol and drugs'. A better expression would be 'alcohol and other drugs' – or just 'drugs' – because alcohol *is* a drug.

Our society marginalizes most kinds of drug-taking, but with alcohol the roles are reversed: people question why you *don't* take it. If you don't drink in this society many people assume you're a bit of a freak.

WHAT KIND OF DRINKER ARE YOU?

Maybe you're a normal drinker who's had one too many hangovers. You might suspect that you're a problem drinker, or you might know full well that you're an alcoholic. Whatever kind of drinker you are, you must have picked up this book for a reason.

Whether you're seeking to control alcohol, or aiming to quit completely, you are holding the answer — providing you follow six simple instructions.

You might find this an extravagant claim, but surely it's worth investigating. If I'm wrong, you will have wasted the price of a couple of drinks and a few hours' drinking time. If I'm right, your troubles with drink are over.

HERE ARE THE FIRST FOUR INSTRUCTIONS:

1) Follow all the instructions.
2) Read the book only when you are sober.
3) Read the book in strict order, from beginning to end.
4) Unless you've already quit for a few days or more, do not attempt to abstain from alcohol or cut down until you've read and understood the whole book.

Think of the solution to your dilemma as a priceless treasure kept in a safe. Here are the numbers that will open the safe:

293658

How confident do you feel that you could get at the treasure?

BUT ARE THEY IN THE RIGHT ORDER?

I just gave you the numbers. I didn't tell you what order they should go in.

The combination that will open the safe is 265839: same numbers, different sequence.

Picture each instruction as one of those numbers. Ignore just one instruction, or take just one out of sequence, and the safe won't open. For example, if you were to try and quit or cut down before completing the book, you would almost certainly feel deprived at some point, and fail.

KEEP AN OPEN MIND

The chances are you assumed the numbers to the combination were in the correct order. But then we're always making assumptions.

Here are the two remaining instructions:

5) Question your assumptions about alcohol.
6) Be positive.

A pessimist sees the bottle as half empty, an optimist as half full. It's two ways of seeing the same thing. Since optimists tend to be happy, you may as well choose to see it as half full. You have nothing to lose and everything to gain.

The real question is: what is *in* the bottle? What is alcohol?

ALCOHOL IS A DIURETIC

A diuretic is a drink that makes you thirsty. That's why you wake at 3 a.m. after a binge with a mouth like a dry riverbed, and one thing on your mind: water! If alcohol quenched thirst the last thing you would need, after all that liquid, is even more. The fact that some people can drink 16 pints of beer proves that alcohol creates thirst: you couldn't drink 16 pints of water if you tried!

IT'S NEVER THE ALCOHOL THAT QUENCHES THIRST OR TASTES GOOD

If an alcoholic drink temporarily quenches your thirst it's not the alcohol that does it, but the water content of that drink.

The same principle applies to taste: if an alcoholic drink tastes good it's not the alcohol, but either the remnant of fruit juice that hasn't turned to alcohol, or the fruit mixer or sugary drink that's been added.

We wouldn't need to sweeten the pill like that if the alcohol itself tasted good.

ALCOHOL IS A POISON

It is produced by letting fruit or other vegetable matter decay, which is why I find it somewhat absurd when wine merchants describe their wares as 'flirtatious', 'cheeky', or 'approachable'. They're talking about a powerful poison! Half a pint of pure alcohol would kill you. Why do you think it makes people vomit? Throwing up might not be particularly pleasant, but don't knock it – it saves your life!

THE HIGHER THE ALCOHOL CONTENT OF A DRINK, THE HARDER IT IS TO GET DOWN

That's why you can guzzle beer but not whisky.

I accept that if you're persistent you can even acquire the taste for neat whisky. But if you're anything like me, you can probably remember grimacing at your very first taste of alcohol. A few years later I was knocking the stuff back like it was going out of style. But the taste *itself* never changed. It was my perception of the taste that altered.

THE TASTE DOESN'T EXPLAIN WHY WE KEEP DOING IT

I enjoy bananas, but if I overindulged in them and woke the following morning with a throbbing head and a sudden need to be sick, I wouldn't repeat the exercise the very same day. If bananas caused me half the problems alcohol did, I'd never go near another banana in my life!

Alcohol must have caused you a few problems, or you wouldn't have started this book. Do you really believe you're putting yourself through all this hassle purely for the taste?

Don't you think the fact that alcohol is an addictive drug might have something to do with it?

ALCOHOL IS A DRUG

It is an anaesthetic and a depressant, and it inebriates.

My dictionary defines inebriation as being 'deprived of the ordinary use of the senses and reason'. In fact alcohol affects all our faculties, including self-control.

Most normal people have a checkpoint between brain and mouth that keeps them out of trouble. Alcohol short-circuits this: it reduces inhibition. This is the very worst thing about it. It's what makes people indulge in phoney displays of affection to complete strangers in the pub, and then go home and shout abuse at their loved ones.

'IT'S JUST THE DRINK TALKING!'

Many people use alcohol as a social lubricant, and you might think there's nothing wrong with having a few drinks to loosen your tongue at social occasions. But while alcohol might make you feel like you're being absolutely fascinating, it's not necessarily true.

Listen to a drunken conversation, but do so when you're sober. You'll realize just how interesting you become when inebriated.

A CURE FOR SHYNESS

If I ever feel self-conscious these days, I try and forget my shyness and help other people overcome theirs. Ask about their job or kids. They'll think you're a great conversationalist, when you've hardly said a word! And there's no hangover!

If you're so shy that my suggestion fills you with horror, take comfort in this: shyness can be a very attractive quality. I'd far rather spend time with someone who's a bit shy than listen to the hollow boasts of some sweaty drunk all puffed up with a sense of his own importance.

ARE WE EVER FOOLED BY DRUNKS?

Do we regard them as go-getting types, facing up to life's big challenges? Or do we see them as rather like one of those normally timid little men who hog the road once they're cocooned in the safety of a big car?

When some usually meek individual drunkenly abuses the waiter over some insignificant detail, do you think, 'I never realized what's-his-name was so assertive!'? When that person from accounts starts dancing half-naked on the table at the office Christmas bash, do you think, 'What a free spirit! I wish *I* was like that!'?

DUTCH COURAGE

Do you actually want the kind of 'confidence' that alcohol creates?

The sad thing is that it's completely false, and everyone knows it. The trouble with using alcohol in this way is that you are telling yourself your inner resources don't exist. For example, if you resort to 'Dutch' courage, you are telling yourself that you lack real courage. After a while you start to believe it, and behave as if it were true.

GENUINE COURAGE

My dictionary defines courage as 'acting *despite* fear'.

Is an ostrich being courageous by sticking its head in the sand at the first sign of danger?

No, it's removing fear; which is a very different thing from conquering it.

In certain situations alcohol could temporarily reduce fear – in which case less genuine courage would be required. Therefore resorting to alcohol in such a situation would actually prevent you from summoning the full force of your own inner courage.

SIGHT, FIGHT AND FLIGHT

You might ask, 'If it helps me face the music, what does it matter if I rely on alcohol rather than my own courage in sticky situations?'

But courage is like a muscle: the more you use it, the stronger it gets.

Besides, by burying its head the ostrich does much more than just remove its fear; it deprives itself of three other faculties essential for survival: the ability to see, to fight and to flee.

Getting drunk *might* reduce fear in certain situations. It will certainly impair your eyesight and coordination. Hence the expressions 'blind drunk' and 'legless'.

FLYING THROUGH FOG

Driving in fog is alarming, even at the slowest speed in daylight. Imagine what it must be like to fly a plane through a mountain range in night-time fog. Now try and imagine what it would be like if the pilot suddenly realized his radar, altimeter, fuel gauge and compass were malfunctioning.

But can you imagine the pilot deliberately tampering with those instruments, so they give false readings? He's flying through fog in a range where he knows the peaks reach 4,000 feet. His altimeter registers the plane's altitude at 2,000 feet: so he adjusts its calibration so that it reads 5,000 feet.

Wouldn't you see that as rather ostrich-like behaviour? But that is effectively what we're doing when we consume alcohol.

I said earlier that in certain situations, alcohol could reduce fear. But if you knew the situation required you to employ your mental and/or physical faculties, the fear would be increased. Why? Because while an ostrich might fool itself by burying its head in the sand, the pilot would know that by interfering with his instrument panel he would be placing himself in even greater danger. So in his case the fear would be magnified. The only way the pilot could remove his fear would be to take action: to increase his altitude.

SURVIVAL OF THE SPECIES

In fact ostriches do not bury their heads during times of danger. Any species that adopted such a stupid tactic would be highly unlikely to survive.

We are completely dependent on our senses and instincts. We think of fear, inhibitions, stress and nerves as evils, but they are vital components of our instinctive survival mechanism. Use a drug to meddle with them and you are embarking on a course as suicidal as the pilot who tinkers with his altimeter.

LOST SOULS?

There are people born without normal instincts: without inhibitions and fear, without any qualms about harming themselves or others. They act like the worst kind of drunk, even when they are sober. Most of them are in institutions, for their own good and that of society.

There are also people born without senses: completely blind, stone deaf, and with no sense of taste, touch or smell.

Would you envy such a person?

Would you get in a car with a blind driver at the wheel?

THE REALITY GAP

But disabled people are aware of their limitations, and adjust accordingly – whereas even small amounts of alcohol impair your faculties, and more than you realise at the time. For many years I was one of those morons that are convinced they drive better after a few drinks – when clearly the reverse is true. Alcohol has a similar effect on wit: everyone thinks they're Oscar Wilde when drunk, when in fact they're just repetitive and incoherent.

This effect is not limited to driving and social skills: alcohol makes you feel more competent in *every* department, while rendering you far less so.

Are you going to go through the rest of your life like that?

A DEADLY COMBINATION

Alcohol places people in dangerous situations, while reducing awareness of that risk. Driving while drunk is just one example. Let's look at another.

A teenage girl walking back from a nightclub should be wary of the approach of strangers. A drunk girl wouldn't have this advantage, so she'd be more likely to accept a lift from a suspect individual. If something ghastly did happen, she would also be far less able to defend herself – and she would know it.

More often than not, when potential danger turns into actual danger, fear is no longer diminished by alcohol but greatly increased.

I DON'T JUST MEAN THE PHYSICAL RISKS

Let's say you're worried because you made a mistake at work. So on the way home you stop off for a few drinks to take your mind off the problem. But while you're in the pub you get a call from your boss saying he or she wants you back in the office straight away to remedy the situation.

At that point your anxiety would be increased, because you would know that in your incapacitated state you would be less capable of solving the problem. You would also have to go through that embarrassing farce of pretending to be more sober than you in fact are, when it is obvious to all concerned that you are considerably the worse for wear.

THE DRUGS DON'T WORK

Can you think of a single instance where aclohol genuinely solved a problem?

A good night's sleep won't solve your problems either. But it will recharge your batteries, help you get the situation in perspective, and leave you more able to tackle it. Getting drunk will run down your batteries and make molehills seem like mountains.

Examine your acquaintances. Who are some of the most stressed and nervous? Aren't they the people who use drugs such as alcohol and nicotine to try and cope with stress and nerves?

But a little bit of stress and nerves can be useful as a stimulus to take action.

THE HUMAN SECURITY SYSTEM

We treat nerves as if they were a disease, rather than a healthy faculty of a fully functional human being. If the door slams and we jump, we tend to say, 'Oh! My nerves are bad!'

That's a sign that your nerves are good.

And stress is no more evil than a fire alarm. If you're worried about something, that's an early warning signal.

It was your anxiety about your drinking that made you pick up this book; and this is the most important point of all. If alcohol were making you confident, brave, calm and relaxed, do you think you'd be reading this book?

PUTTING OUT FIRE WITH GASOLINE

Alcohol takes the edge off inhibitions, fear, nerves and stress the night before – only to magnify them the morning after.

As I used to say to people, 'If you had my problems, you'd drink as much as me.' It cut me to the bone when a true friend replied, 'If I drank as much as you, I'd have your problems.' But thank you Steve, because those few words saved my life!

This is the key to understanding the illusion of relaxation.

DO YOU BELIEVE ALCOHOL RELAXES YOU?

When some drunken yob is threatening people with a broken bottle, what is your initial reaction? Is it, 'Quick! Give him another drink to calm him down!'?

The yob is acting like that because alcohol has deadened whatever sense of responsibility he had, and it is the deadening effect of alcohol that creates the illusion of relaxation. It doesn't solve your problems; it just temporarily dulls your anxiety about them.

But it's alcohol that creates most of the problems in the first place.

It's like banging your head so hard against the wall that eventually you'll pass out, and be unaware of the pain.

PUNCH-DRUNK?

Actually the last analogy is particularly appropriate, because the behaviour of a drunk is very like that of someone with brain damage.

The word 'anaesthesia' means the absence of feeling or sensation. How can an anaesthetic genuinely relax you? Take enough of this drug and you'll lose all consciousness: is that relaxation?

Is a boxer who has been knocked out cold genuinely relaxed?

Well he is oblivious to his problems, but that's not the same thing. It's impossible to feel relaxed – or indeed to feel anything – if you're unconscious.

TRUE RELAXATION IS NOT SOME DAZED STUPOR!

Perhaps you can see that drinking yourself into a coma doesn't solve anything, but feel that moderate alcohol consumption helps you relax.

So let's say the boxer is not out for the count, but still reeling around, stunned and confused. Is *that* relaxation?

No: if being unconscious is not genuinely relaxing, then neither is being semi-conscious. It doesn't matter how much or how little alcohol you consume, because true mental relaxation is in fact an alert state. It isn't trying to block out cares and worries, it's feeling completely free of them.

'BUT THERE'S NOT A PERSON ON THE PLANET THAT NEVER HAS CARES OR WORRIES!'

True: but we can have *moments* of complete calm. You'll find those few and far between if you seek refuge in a bottle.

Wouldn't it be better to think up a solution? Alcohol won't help you do that!

Nor will it completely take your mind off your problems. It's not a particularly effective anaesthetic, so unless you *do* drink yourself into a coma you're stuck with a certain amount of anxiety, even while you're inebriated. When I suffered from fear of flying it didn't matter how much I drank, I would feel stone-cold sober when the plane took off – and still terrified.

IF ALCOHOL WERE AN EFFECTIVE ANAESTHETIC THEY WOULD USE IT IN HOSPITALS

Alcohol gets even less effective as you develop tolerance. Tolerance is the process of building up resistance to alcohol, so it becomes increasingly ineffective at taking your mind off the problems it creates.

Test it out. Make a note of your current biggest worry. It might be your drink problem itself. Between now and completing the book, while you're having a few drinks, take a look at that note. Do you feel blissfully free of the problem?

How have we all been fooled into believing that an anaesthetic, depressant drug is a genuine crutch and a pleasure?

IT HAPPENS BY OSMOSIS

An infant brain is as receptive as a sponge, and children tend to absorb many of the beliefs, opinions and prejudices of the adults around them. This applies to alcohol as much as to anything else.

Most of us are shocked by news reports about teenage drinking. But is it any wonder that our kids are attracted to this drug? Most adults take it, and must get some benefit from taking it – or so the youngster presumes.

We don't *make* assumptions about booze; we inherit them from the culture in which we are raised.

UNDER THE INFLUENCE

When I was young, Hollywood played the main role in selling the illusion: those glamorous leading ladies invariably had a Martini in one hand and a cigarette in the other, and every action hero had a taste for rot-gut whisky.

These days there are so many forms of media that we are susceptible to manipulation even in the comfort of our own homes.

We may have been influenced by our relations, our peers, TV, movies, or glossy magazines. But from an early age most of us bought into an *image* of alcohol: we swallowed the idea that to drink is to be adult, sophisticated and sexy.

DOUBLE STANDARDS

But it's a mixed message that we get from society. People who drink 'too much' are frowned upon, and teenagers receive endless lectures about the horrors of addiction and the dangers of alcohol 'abuse'– often from people who are themselves no strangers to the bottle.

If you feel you enjoyed your first few drinks it was probably the psychological kick of playing with fire, the sweet taste of rebellion, or the feeling of finally being a member of a very grown-up club.

RITES OF PASSAGE

I was brought up in a social environment in which there were three really significant events in a young lad's life: losing your virginity; passing your driving test; and that first pint of bitter on your sixteenth birthday, watched over by your beaming father and his pub cronies. These days it's more likely to be a glass of wine at home, but alcohol remains the one drug that many parents actively encourage their children to take.

THE EMPEROR'S NEW CLOTHES

By the time the novelty of alcohol consumption has started to wear thin, we've already developed a degree of tolerance. It's much easier to kid yourself that something is pleasant when it doesn't seem quite so unpleasant. It's also much easier when everyone else is kidding themselves too.

The alcohol industry spends astronomical sums of money persuading us to see alcohol in a certain light, but the most influential source of advertising will always be other drinkers. Since 90 per cent of the adult population drinks, that's a pretty powerful sales force.

THE FABRIC OF SOCIETY IS SOAKED IN BOOZE

It is consumed at births, christenings, Easter, Christmas, birthdays, graduation ceremonies, weddings and funerals. A social event without alcohol? It sounds like a contradiction in terms! But with the exception of funerals, these are all extremely pleasant occasions in their own right. If a group of friends are enjoying themselves at a birthday celebration or in a bar, it's not because they're consuming alcohol! It's because they're having a laugh with people whose company they enjoy.

There's exactly the same atmosphere in the changing room before a football match, when no alcohol has been consumed.

'WIN OR LOSE, HIT THE BOOZE!'

When the match is over, does the winning team need alcohol to be happy? No: they're on a genuine high from the final whistle. Often they don't even drink the champagne, they spray it over each other instead!

Does the atmosphere in the losers' changing-room switch from gloom to delight when they have a drink? Or does alcohol – the depressant – make them even more depressed?

IS IT THE ALCOHOL THAT CREATES THE MOOD – OR THE SITUATION IN WHICH IT IS CONSUMED?

When I was an accountant I'd get home from work, put some music on, grab a drink and put my feet up. I'd take one sip and let out a long sigh of relief – *long before the drug had had time to take effect.*

But coming home from a hard day's work is extremely pleasant anyway!

It's not the alcohol we enjoy, but the scenario in which it is consumed. The alcohol seems pleasant by association.

TRY THIS EXPERIMENT

Prove it to yourself. Separate the experience of inebriation from anything that might influence your perception of it. Spend an evening alone in an empty room with plenty of your usual tipple, but no diversions such as TV, books or music – nothing to distract you from the feeling of being drunk.

See how much fun you have.

But if it were the alcohol itself that gave pleasure, it would be as enjoyable in an empty room as in a pub full of laughter.

THE ICING ON THE CAKE?

Almost all the situations in which we consume alcohol are enjoyable in themselves: the end of the working day, the Friday night meal in a restaurant, parties, romantic dinners, Saturday night down the pub with friends.

But surely alcohol makes good times even better? Surely it adds to the love-making by the fire? Surely it enhances the appreciation of music?

Does it?

AN ANAESTHETIC IS A DRUG THAT KILLS FEELING

Alcohol dulls the brain to pain and pleasure alike.

But drinkers will believe anything. They somehow manage to convince themselves that alcohol is some kind of smart bomb: that it wipes out trouble and woe, but miraculously leaves pleasant experiences intact. It just doesn't work like that. If you use alcohol to take the edge off your cares and worries, there's going to be collateral damage: it will take the edge off genuine pleasures as well.

IT'S A CON!

We've all been led to believe that an adult social function is incomplete without booze. But before you first consumed the stuff you could enjoy yourself without it. Children don't need it. They can have a great time at parties on nothing stronger than lemonade. Ten per cent of adults are perfectly capable of having a good time without alcohol. Actually so are the other 90 per cent! You must be able to remember at least one occasion when you had a wonderful evening, and little or no alcohol was consumed.

THE ILLUSION OF PLEASURE

It's not true that you can't have a good time without booze. But if you believe you won't be able to enjoy a certain occasion without a drink, you'll be miserable until you get one. Get hold of a drink and you'll be able to enjoy an occasion that the non-drinker can enjoy anyway. If you already know (or even suspect) that you've got a drink problem, the pleasure of the occasion will be tarnished by that knowledge.

Alcohol takes the icing off the cake, and hands a few crumbs back to create the illusion of pleasure.

Wouldn't you prefer to be fully present for every human experience? Why not show up for the one life you've got?

WHAT IS SO GREAT ABOUT BEING 'OUT OF IT'?

The expressions we use for drunkenness are highly significant. Many are references to bodily functions: for example 'bladdered', along with others I could mention; or they refer to the fact that alcohol impairs every one of your faculties: 'blind drunk', 'legless', and 'paralytic'; or the images are of violence, destruction and death: 'bombed', 'hammered', 'blitzed', 'slaughtered', 'smashed', 'trashed', 'mashed', 'annihilated', 'wrecked', and most revealing of all, 'wasted'.

MY MEDICAL DICTIONARY USES SLIGHTLY DIFFERENT LANGUAGE

It defines the effects of alcohol as: 'deterioration of intellectual and motor functions; lengthening of reaction time; dulling of higher mental processes; impairment of judgement, attention, self-discipline, co-ordinating skills and visual acuity; and decreasing sensitivity to sensory stimuli'.

A FRESH PERSPECTIVE?

Imagine what the effects of alcohol would be like to someone who has never heard of it: who has never been brainwashed or warned about those effects, and has never had a chance to build up some tolerance to them. Imagine they were tricked into consuming a large amount, and suddenly found themselves unable to think, move, see or talk properly!

Do you think it would be pleasant – or just very, very scary?

Since being completely sloshed would be extremely unpleasant for such a person, does it not follow that being slightly inebriated would be mildly unpleasant?

WHO'S MORE LIKELY TO BE THINKING 'OUTSIDE THE BOX'?

Most teetotallers don't drink because the prospect of losing control – to any degree – holds absolutely no appeal for them. If they do try alcohol their beliefs are usually confirmed: they find both the taste and effect unpleasant. Many kids have a healthy suspicion of alcohol and ask: 'Why do adults do it?'

The only people who are convinced it is pleasant are drinkers.

DIFFERENT VIEWPOINTS

Perhaps you feel non-drinkers are goody two-shoes who wouldn't know a good time if it slapped them in the face. That's an opinion shared by many drinkers – at least while they're drunk.

But is that how you feel when you're sober and someone else is smashed?

When you see some drunken lout reeling around in the street, do they look like they're enjoying themselves?

When do you think you're more likely to see inebriation for what it really is: when your judgement has been impaired by a drug, or when you are on the outside looking in?

AN INSTANT CURE

Go into any British town centre on a Friday or Saturday night, but do it when you're sober. You'll see alcohol for what it is! Virtually everyone is plastered! Normally sensible individuals are doing incredibly stupid things – things they wouldn't dream of doing if they were sober. Do they really look like they're having a better time because they're drunk?

I HATE TO SPOIL THE PARTY, BUT...

Seventy per cent of UK admissions to Accident and Emergency departments on a Saturday night are alcohol-related. A recent survey shows that alcohol is a significant factor in forty-four per cent of all violent crime, and forty-two per cent of domestic violence. In a study of men imprisoned for rape, seventy per cent admitted they'd been drinking prior to the crime. Over twenty per cent of murders are alcohol-related. The official figure is that approximately one thousand suicides a year are linked to alcohol. I imagine the real figure is far higher. And what of the people left behind?

Alcohol causes more human suffering than all other drugs combined.

A BALANCED ACCOUNT

I have emphasized the disadvantages of alcohol, so I
shall now cover its benefits.

THE BENEFITS OF ALCOHOL

1. It can be used as an antiseptic.
2. It is a powerful detergent.
3. It can be burnt as a fuel.

DRINKING ALCOHOL PROVIDES NO BENEFITS WHATSOEVER

Let's return to the aeroplane analogy.

Imagine being a passenger on that flight through the fog, and watching the pilot swigging from his hip-flask!

So why is it OK to do it to yourself? You're the pilot of your plane. The human body is a highly complex machine. It automatically supplies adrenalin and other substances, when we need them and in the quantities that we need. As for your brain, it is a far more sophisticated computer than anything you'll find in the most modern aeroplane.

Do you really believe you can improve on something that ingenious by taking a chemical that radically affects its proper functioning?

BUT WE ARE MORE THAN MERE MACHINES RUN BY COMPUTERS

The resourcefulness of the human spirit never ceases to amaze me. Look around you! Every single day so-called 'ordinary' people act with astonishing heroism, and they're not using alcohol to do it.

THE TWO LIES

The alcohol trap consists of two lies so outrageous that it is quite staggering that 90 per cent of the adult population have swallowed them whole without question. The first is that human beings are weak and incomplete in some way, and the second is that alcohol makes up for this supposed deficiency.

It's like someone who hasn't got a broken leg buying a crutch that's riddled with woodworm.

INSIDE THE PITCHER PLANT: PART ONE

If there are no benefits to drinking alcohol, then are normal drinkers in control of their situation?

Have you seen a pitcher plant? It is shaped like a pitcher, or vase. The scent of its nectar attracts flies, which alight on the lip of the vase and sip the nectar. The slope at the top is so slight that the fly doesn't realize it is being gradually lured downwards. By the time the slope has become steeper, the fly is too preoccupied with the nectar to notice. When it gets just beyond the neck of the vase, it can see many dead insects in a pool of liquid at the bottom. But it knows it can fly away whenever it likes. So it feels quite safe continuing to gorge on the nectar. By the time it's had enough and decides to fly off, it's too bloated to do so. The fly panics; and the more it struggles to escape, the more it covers itself in the sticky nectar, which weighs it down even more, and makes it impossible for it to get a grip on the sides of the plant, which are now vertical.

The liquid at the bottom is not nectar, but the digestive juice of the plant.

LOSS OF CONTROL: PART ONE

When did the fly lose control?

It must have been before it slid into the digestive juice.

Was it when it tried to escape and found it couldn't?

No: that was when it realized it had lost control, so it must have been before then.

Was it when it saw all the dead insects at the bottom of the plant?

Or was it at some point on the gradual slope at the top?

THE ILLUSION OF CONTROL: PART ONE

At either of those stages the fly could have escaped, had it wanted to.

But it *didn't* want to, because it didn't realize it was in a trap.

The fly was never in control. It was being subtly controlled by the plant from the moment it got a whiff of the nectar.

INSIDE THE PITCHER PLANT: PART TWO

From a tender age we are led to believe that alcohol is the nectar for humans. So let's apply this analogy to a real-life case: that of Fred, a chronic alcoholic on Skid Row.

Fred didn't begin his drinking career on a bottle of meths a day: he worked up to it from a seemingly harmless start. So let's track his progress to rock bottom.

His first alcoholic drink was a shandy at a teenage disco. In his twenties Fred was 'one of the lads', believing he enjoyed a drink and that it could never be a problem. He got a scare in his thirties, when his old drinking buddy was treated for alcoholism. But Fred reassured himself that if *he* ever got that bad he'd just stop. In his forties a number of embarrassing incidents culminated in Fred's arrest for drunk-driving. So he tried to stop. The trouble was he believed he was 'giving up' a genuine crutch and a pleasure. When he inevitably caved in and went on a ten-day bender, he realized he had a very serious problem indeed. The sheer panic drove him deeper into the bottle; he soon lost his job, friends and family, and within a few short years he was drinking meths on the street.

LOSS OF CONTROL: PART TWO

There are various definitions of addiction, but loss of control is not a bad one.

So when did Fred lose control?

It must have been before he started drinking meths.

Was it during his futile attempt to 'give up'?

No: that was when he realized he had lost control, so it must have been before then.

Was it when the friend was treated for alcoholism?

Or was it at some point during Fred's 'one of the lads' period?

THE ILLUSION OF CONTROL: PART TWO

Many people will argue that Fred was still in control at both those stages, because he could have stopped and averted the disaster that followed.

But he *didn't* stop, nor did he have any desire to, because he couldn't see the disaster coming.

Grasp that, and you will realize that Fred lost control the moment he took his very first alcoholic drink.

THE BIGGER PICTURE

For many years Fred looked like he was in control, told everyone he was in control, and believed it himself. But like the fly in the pitcher plant, he was being subtly controlled from his first-ever sip.

Normal drinkers are in exactly the same position. OK, most die before alcohol completely wrecks their lives. Bully for them! There's an insidious way in which all drinkers are sliding down the alcohol pit, regardless of the amount they drink.

NORMAL DRINKERS AND ALCOHOLICS DRINK FOR SIMILAR REASONS

Alcoholics just start earlier in the day!

All drinkers must believe this drug provides a genuine crutch and/or pleasure, or they wouldn't take it. But the ability to face life and the capacity for fun don't come in a bottle! These things come from inside, and nothing can replace them. If a person is trying to use any amount of alcohol instead of those inner resources, they are telling themselves those resources don't exist. It's not true – but if you believe it, it might as well be!

DEATH BY A THOUSAND CUTS

If you find it hard to believe that booze is gradually eroding a normal drinker's courage and enjoyment of life, it's for the same reason they can't see it: it's precisely *because* it happens so gradually. This is the most deceptive thing about the slide down the alcohol pit: we don't notice it happening day by day. It's only when we look back that we're shocked at how far we have slid. Even then we tend not to blame the true culprit, but the ageing process, or the circumstances of our lives.

It all happens so slowly that we think it's normal.

THAT FATAL FIRST SIP

Most flies slide down the pitcher plant at roughly the same rate: pretty rapidly. Therefore it is obvious that any fly entering the plant is in very real danger. The teenager sipping their first pint is in just as much danger, but it's far from obvious, because most people slide down the alcohol pit very slowly; so slowly that they appear to be getting away with it.

WHY DO PEOPLE SLIDE AT DIFFERENT RATES?

Because every victim is unique. The rate at which an individual slides depends on countless factors: where you were raised; the general attitude to alcohol and the degree of availability; whether your parents and friends drank and encouraged you to join them; the nature of your career. Strong, dynamic people tend to slide much faster: you have to be pretty tough in mind and body to take the punishment.

APPLYING THE BRAKES

Remember that most drinkers have powerful reasons not to slide faster: they have families, reputations and lives to maintain. Not to mention careers: most people have to get up in the morning and go to work. You could argue that Fred had all these things too, and they didn't stop him sliding faster. But the difference between Fred and a normal drinker is that Fred *realized* he had a problem – whereupon alcohol acquired all the irresistible appeal of forbidden fruit.

THE CRITICAL POINT

There's a point in the alcohol pit where the drinker senses they're hooked, panics, and tries to control their drinking. That just makes alcohol seem all the more precious in the victim's mind. They are now in the truly agonizing position of wanting to drink more *and* less at the same time. Like the fly in the pitcher plant they struggle; and the struggle accelerates their descent. Society labels those above the critical point as 'normal' or 'social' drinkers, and those below it as 'problem' drinkers or 'alcoholics'.

SOCIETY'S LABELS

Most people would accept without question that there are several different types of drinker: 'normal drinkers', 'social drinkers', 'heavy social drinkers', 'binge drinkers', 'problem drinkers', 'alcoholics', and 'chronic alcoholics'. But these are just labels for different stages of descent down the same alcohol pit, and if it weren't for certain restrictions many 'normal' drinkers could very easily progress through some or all of the later stages.

WATCH 'NORMAL' DRINKERS

Watch what happens to many of them when one of these restrictions is removed, for instance when the person who would never drink and drive is offered a lift home. The chances are they'll get absolutely hammered! Watch what happens when someone who can't afford to drink more gets a pay rise. Watch the career-minded – who would never drink in the week – when they hit the weekend! Watch people on holiday, particularly a holiday where free drinks are part of the package, and the usual restrictions of balancing the budget, work, and 'what will the neighbours think?' are temporarily suspended.

MANY PEOPLE START DRINKING AFTER BREAKFAST ON HOLIDAY!

Morning drinking is universally recognized as a sign of a serious problem. So do these supposedly 'normal' drinkers suddenly become 'problem' drinkers on holiday, and revert to being 'normal' drinkers back home?

I accept that many 'normal' drinkers never get drunk, even on holiday. That's because they can't see anything that great about getting smashed out of their minds. And they're absolutely right! It's a horrible thing to have to do to yourself! But they must believe they get *something* from this drug, or they wouldn't consume it at all.

LISTEN TO 'NORMAL' DRINKERS

I shouldn't try and make much sense out of what they say. Focus instead on why they bother to say it. You know the sort of thing: 'Frankly I can take it or leave it. Sometimes I go a month without a drink.'

Imagine I said, 'Frankly I can take them or leave them. Sometimes I go a month without a banana.'

Would you think, 'Allen obviously hasn't got a problem with bananas!', or the exact opposite? What's so special about going a month without a banana – unless you've got a very serious banana problem indeed?

GOING ON THE WAGON FOR A MONTH

The drinker is trying to prove that they haven't got a problem. They're proving the opposite. If they believe they enjoy a drink, why bother to go a month without one? Obviously because their drinking is causing them problems. And if they really can take it or leave it, why start drinking again and return to the problem? Equally obvious: it's a lie that they can take it or leave it. They're *not* happy taking it but they *can't* leave it. They've been conned into believing this drug provides benefits, so they feel incomplete without it. There's no better definition of alcohol addiction than that.

'NORMAL' DRINKERS PROTEST TOO MUCH

Many of their 'months on the wagon' are aborted attempts to quit completely, in disguise. If they tell people they're quitting for good and then fail, everyone will know they're hooked. Better to keep their options open. That way they can disguise their failure as success. Hence the smug, 'I can go a month without a drink'; or, 'I never have a third drink'; or, 'I never drink spirits/in the week/before six'; and so on. When I had an alcohol problem I was too worried about my own drinking to notice that 'normal' drinkers break their rules as often as they keep them. But why would they need to try and regulate their drinking if they hadn't experienced problems due to alcohol? And why do they need to tell you about it?

They are trying to make themselves feel better about their own alcohol consumption, by making you feel worse about yours.

You might have noticed that many 'normal' drinkers have to have an *angle* on their drinking, the most popular being:

'I ONLY DO IT TO BE SOCIABLE'

… not 'I enjoy it,' which if it were the true reason wouldn't even need to be stated – because we seldom feel the need to defend genuine pleasures.

If I told you that I only played football to be sociable, I would be telling you that I didn't enjoy playing football.

Likewise, if a drinker clutches at a rationalization such as, 'I only do it to be sociable', it proves that they don't genuinely enjoy drinking. It also indicates that they sense they've got a problem.

SAFETY IN NUMBERS

Alcohol is the only drink which people *insist* you share with them, even after you've refused twice.

Imagine declining a pineapple juice, to which your host replies:

'Oh, go on.'

'No, thank you.'

'Oh, go on!'

'No, really, I'm fine!'

'Oh, don't be anti-social!'

Drinkers find that even the illusion of pleasure disappears if they are the only ones doing it.

IT'S THE OCCASION THAT IS SOCIABLE

But have I never heard of the local pub? Of course: but you can be sociable at the pub without drinking alcohol. It's yet another example of confusing alcohol with the situation in which it is consumed. Alcohol is a drug: nothing more, nothing less. Some people happen to take it on social occasions, some don't. Some people smoke on social occasions, some don't. Are the non-smokers being anti-social because they don't smoke? Are the smokers being more sociable because they do?

Are drinkers being more sociable because they are consuming a poison?

WHAT COULD BE MORE ANTI-SOCIAL THAN ANAESTHETIZING YOURSELF IN OTHER PEOPLE'S COMPANY?

The implication is that the only way you can bear to be in their presence is by numbing your brain.

You have two huge advantages over a 'normal' or 'social' drinker: you know you've got a problem, and you've decided to do something about it. That's why you picked up this book.

Before you decide what you are going to do about it, I'd like you to reflect on something.

DID YOU MAKE A FREE CHOICE TO BECOME A DRINKER?

Let me use an analogy. Did you choose to start speaking English – or did you just copy those around you?

Isn't that a bit like drinking alcohol?

When you picked up your very first drink, did you decide that eventually you would take this drug every week or even every day?

When you were an innocent kid – your whole life ahead of you – was this what you had planned?

Did you choose to have a drink problem?

But you *can* choose to solve it. When will that be?

When life gets a bit less stressful?

TOMORROW NEVER COMES

Please don't fall for that trick. It's the most sinister element of the trap, and it will keep you hooked for the rest of your days – if you let it. Life never gets less stressful on drugs. On the contrary, it gets progressively more so, because the drugs create most of the stress.

It takes courage to decide to do something about your drinking. Nonetheless I want you to do that now. Before you read on, take a moment to make the decision to do whatever it takes to solve your problem. Don't worry: you have absolutely nothing to lose. If you follow my suggestions you will find it easy and enjoyable, and your life will improve beyond measure!

THINK ABOUT THE FANTASTICALLY UNLIKELY FACT OF YOUR EXISTENCE

Your life is a vital link in a never-ending chain of events, and if any one of the coincidences that led to your birth hadn't taken place in exactly the way it did, you would not be here. Maybe painful things have happened to you. But trying to escape into a bottle creates even more pain, and you must know that, or you wouldn't still be reading.

Alcohol doesn't make a difficult world bearable, it turns an intensely beautiful world into a living hell.

YOU'VE HAD THE GUTS TO COME THIS FAR – IN THE BOOK AND IN YOUR LIFE

If you've mucked up the portion of your life that's already elapsed with booze, *please* don't use that as an excuse to do the same with the precious remainder! It's never too late to turn over a new leaf. But it's never too soon either. This might be your last chance to solve your drink problem.

You will soon be making a decision about whether you are going to try and cut down, or quit completely. Before you do, let's look at whether cutting down is a desirable goal.

IS CUTTING DOWN DESIRABLE?

Perhaps you can see that getting completely plastered doesn't solve anything, but still feel alcohol provides benefits in moderation.

But either the effects of this drug are beneficial, or they aren't.

How would you feel if the pilot of your plane said, 'We're about to fly over some mountains. There's thick fog outside. When I look at my altimeter and it tells me we've only got 20 feet clearance, I get a bit scared. I'm sure you won't mind if I tweak the calibration ever so slightly, so it tells me we've got 50 feet clearance.'?

It doesn't matter how deep you bury your head in the sand, it's always a dumb thing to do.

IT'S SO OBVIOUS WITH OTHER DRUGS

Most people know it's a bad idea to take any amount of heroin.

If you're thinking, 'But injecting is unnatural!' then so is pouring a poison down your throat.

If you're thinking, 'But heroin ruins lives!' ask yourself how many people you know whose lives have been wrecked by heroin. Alcohol kills five people an hour in the UK.

And if you're thinking, 'But heroin's illegal!' ask yourself whether, if they legalized it tomorrow, that would make it OK to take a little bit of heroin at the end of the day.

TREAT THE CAUSE, NOT THE SYMPTOM

Take action. If something's playing on your mind, it's for a reason. Send an e-mail or make a phone call.

There's no time at the end of the working day? Make a note to make the call or send the e-mail in the morning. And then forget about it. That's a skill you can acquire with a bit of practice.

'But it's so much easier to have a drink or two.'

If you believed that you would have stopped reading a long time ago.

YOUR VERY GOOD HEALTH?

But perhaps you believe a little bit of alcohol is good for you.

The main reason for this belief is that certain kinds of alcohol contain antioxidants.

But if you can get antioxidants from alcohol, surely that means there are benefits to consuming it?

Hardly: you *could* use your head to bang a nail into the wall, but would you describe that as one of its benefits, when you could use a hammer instead?

If you want some antioxidants, get them from tomatoes, mangoes, apricots, strawberries, peaches or indeed unfermented grape juice!

THE ROAD TO HELL

Let's assume for a moment that it's better to get your antioxidants from alcohol than fresh fruit, rather than vice versa; and let's imagine your doctor says that for someone of your size and build one drink is good for your health, and two are bad. The trouble is that even one drink will start to affect your self-control, just enough to make you have 'just one more'. That second drink doubles the effect, the third triples it, and by the fourth drink the last thing on what's left of your mind is the good of your health!

IS CUTTING DOWN FEASIBLE?

Some drinkers manage to cut down temporarily. They are usually people whose drinking has given them a real scare, but they cannot conceive of total freedom from alcohol. What you don't see is what it costs them, in terms of mental aggravation, to limit their intake.

Something I often hear from drinkers is, 'I did manage to cut down for a while. It was the most miserable time of my life.'

And it is usually followed by a bender of unprecedented proportions – just as every diet is followed by a binge.

DOES DIETING MAKE FOOD SEEM LESS PRECIOUS?

On the contrary: you obsess about it all day. You're miserable when you can't eat, and miserable when you can, because you can't eat enough!

The same applies with booze: if you were to try and cut down, it would be like trying to diet for the rest of your life. And how long do most diets last?

So if it's that difficult to control your intake of food, can you imagine how hard it would be to try and control the intake of a drug that reduces self-control – *including any self-control you might hope to exercise over drinking?*

BE HONEST

Can you plan to have one or two drinks and *guarantee* it will be just one or two? Or do your best-laid plans tend to go horribly wrong?

There may or may not be negative consequences every single time you drink. But just as one drink leads to another, so one session leads to the next. There must be some pretty bad things happening, some of the time. I doubt you've stayed with me this long purely out of appreciation for the elegance of my prose!

But you cannot possibly get drunk if you don't take the first drink.

ONE AND THE SAME THING

At the start I said that whether you were seeking to control alcohol, or aiming to quit completely, you were holding the answer. If I misled you into believing that cutting down was an option, I make no apologies. My motive was to ensure you complete the book, thereby avoiding years of hell trying to limit your intake.

Otherwise you would have had to learn the hard way – towards the end of a wasted life – that it has to be all or nothing.

There is an easy way to control alcohol. It happens to be the only way: don't drink the stuff at all.

SAME AGAIN, BARMAN

Insanity has been defined as doing the same thing over and over again, and expecting a different result each time. In that case I must have been stark raving mad by the final days of my own drinking, because almost every time I drank I'd consume more than intended, and bad things were happening with depressing regularity.

It would have been boring if it hadn't been so damned painful.

GROUNDHOG DAY

Have you seen this movie? Bill Murray plays a self-centred man, condemned to live the same day over and over and over again.

That's exactly what the tail-end of my drinking career felt like: as if I were stuck in the same horrific day, endlessly repeated. I'd come to and check the extent of my hangover. Breakfast was a fistful of aspirin washed down with black coffee. After breakfast I'd try and piece together the night before – and immediately wish I hadn't. I'd attempt to do some work for about five minutes, give up, and wallow in remorse for a few idle hours. Then I'd try and have just one or two drinks, and fail quite spectacularly. In my drunken stupor I'd fantasize about a more fulfilling life, telling myself that tomorrow would be different. Then I'd pass out. A few hours later I'd come to – and the nightmare would start all over again.

The worst thing is knowing that you're not moving forward as a person.

BUT PERHAPS YOU FEEL GROUNDHOG DAY MIGHT BE QUITE FUN

If there were no tomorrow there would be no consequences to our actions, and at first Bill Murray tries to find satisfaction by exploiting this fact. He overeats and chain-smokes, because he can't possibly put on weight or get cancer. And he drinks like a fish, and does incredibly stupid things while drunk, such as driving on the railway tracks! But it doesn't matter to him, because although he goes to sleep in a police cell, he wakes up in his hotel bed without the slightest hint of a hangover.

A DRINKER'S HEAVEN?

Many drinkers would think of the *Groundhog Day* scenario as heaven on earth, because there would be no repercussions to drinking: no health problems, no missed opportunities or broken relationships, no mumbled apologies and empty promises the morning after – because there would be no morning after.

But there would still be no point in consuming any amount of alcohol. We have all only got one day: this one, today. If it's a bad day, don't try and escape into a bottle! Do something about it. Fix the problem. If that proves impossible, accept it. Either way it stops being a problem.

And if it's a good day, enjoy it to the full!

LIFE BEYOND THE BOTTLE

Bill Murray soon tires of drinking, which makes him even more jaded, cynical and depressed. He loses interest in the bottle and takes an interest in life and other people. And that breaks the spell! He wakes up a changed man, and it's not just the beginning of a new and different day: it's the start of a whole new life.

That was how it felt when I finally decided to quit drinking for good.

That's how it will feel for you, if you make the right decision today.

It is seldom that we can make a decision and be absolutely certain, while we're making it, that it is the correct decision — but this is one of those rare occasions.

Your health and happiness critically depend on this decision.

What could possibly be more important than the length and quality of your future life?

THE FINAL PREPARATION

You should by now be like a dog straining at the leash, desperate to get free. If not, there are two possible explanations:

• You've missed a vital point. You must still believe there are benefits to drinking alcohol. But would you trust your life to a pilot who tampered with his instrument panel?

Re-read the book.

•You've understood everything and are dithering unnecessarily.

In that case just trust me and go for it! What terrible thing will happen if you never take another alcoholic drink?

WHEN IS THE BEST TIME TO GET RID OF A FATAL, PROGRESSIVE DISEASE?

Imagine you had another life-threatening disease, and you heard of an instant, permanent cure. All you have to do is cut one item out of your diet. Would you hesitate to put the cure into effect?

When would you know you were free of the disease forever? Would you wait to get excited about your freedom?

How would you feel about people who were in the very early stages of the same disease but didn't know it? Would you envy them for having the disease?

Would you ever be tempted to give yourself the disease again?

WASTED BREATH

It drives me close to despair when people conjure up these complicated theories about why people get hooked on alcohol. If you've been shot with a poisoned arrow, do you waste time asking who shot it, what direction it came from, and with what kind of poison the arrowhead is tipped? Aren't you more likely to take some action? Wouldn't you remove the arrow as soon as possible?

Alcohol is the one factor common to everyone who has ever had a problem with the stuff. You cannot possibly have an alcohol problem if you don't drink alcohol.

THE FINAL INSTRUCTIONS

Before you take your final drink, here are some final instructions. The previous instructions were to ensure you read the book in the right spirit. These are to guarantee that you remain a happy non-drinker for the rest of your life.

1. Once you've taken your final drink, **don't wait to become a non-drinker**. You will already be a non-drinker. Get out there and enjoy yourself from the start.

2. **Don't change any other aspect of your lifestyle, unless you want to anyway**. If you have genuine friends down the pub, join them. No one's going to force a drink down your throat.

3. **Avoid all substitutes**, whether the substitute is an activity, an item of food, a non-alcoholic drink, or anything else. When you consume drinks that quench rather than create thirst, you won't need a glass of something in your hand all evening. I'm not suggesting you give up eating and drinking! I'm saying: don't use excess food or drinks, or anything else, as a substitute. If a certain activity gives you pleasure, enjoy it to the full! But do it *because* you enjoy it, not as a substitute. By even thinking of using a substitute, you would be telling yourself that you're missing out on something.

4. **Don't try not to think about alcohol**. But whenever you do think about it, think, 'Great! I'm free!'

Do accept that at any point in the future you might unexpectedly get the thought, 'I want a drink.' It might be normal thirst, or simply that you've forgotten you no longer drink. You have a choice. You can say, 'I mustn't have a drink,' and make yourself miserable; or you can say, 'This is just a thought. Isn't it wonderful that I don't have to act on it? I'm a non-drinker!'

5. Any big change can involve a period of adjustment. If you experience any discomfort over the next few days, remind yourself that it's not because you stopped drinking; it's because you started. **Rejoice in the fact that you've just got rid of a horrific disease**.

6. If you take that attitude you will soon experience 'The Moment of Revelation'. This usually comes after an occasion when you previously would have drunk alcohol. You suddenly realize that the thought that you no longer drink barely crossed your mind. But **don't wait for 'The Moment of Revelation'**. You will have achieved your goal the second you finish your final drink.

7. **Don't worry if you do completely forget you've quit**, and absent-mindedly ask the barman for a gin and tonic or a pint. There's nothing to worry about, providing you don't drink it!

8. **Don't make an issue of it if you mistakenly take a sip of someone else's alcoholic drink**. Just make a mental note to be more careful in future, and forget about it. Please don't misunderstand me! I'm not saying that you can get away with the odd tipple! I'm saying that if it's a genuine mistake it couldn't possibly hook you again.

9. There are three main reasons people do get hooked again, and the first is the influence of drinkers. The reason a lobster tank doesn't have a lid is that if a lobster tries to escape, the others claw it back. Drinkers might use various tactics to try and claw you back. Know that it is fear that makes the poor drinker behave like that, and that you are well shot of it. Look them straight in the eye and say, 'I never drink when I'm sober!'

Never envy drinkers. Pity them for what they are: flies at various stages of descent down the pitcher plant. And always remember that in the case of the alcohol trap, the nectar is an illusion.

10. The second main reason for failure is using a bad day as an excuse to drink. Just remember that a drink wouldn't help the situation. On the contrary, it would turn a difficult day into a tragedy. It would turn you back into a drinker, probably for life. **Remind yourself that you had bad days as a drinker**, or you wouldn't have read this book. Maybe things will look very different in the morning. If you want a boost in hard times, use the fact that you *don't* drink as your little prop.

11. The third reason for failure is that people find it so easy to quit that they believe they can get away with 'just one drink', and that even if they don't get away with it, they'll find it easy to quit again.

I could fill another book explaining why the alcohol trap doesn't work like that, so please just **trust me: there is no such thing as 'just one drink'**. Even if there were, when would you drink it? Next year? Twenty years from now? Do you really want to spend the rest of your life waiting for the next dose of poison?

12. Finally, **don't worry if you dream that you're drinking again**. It's common for people who have got free of a drug to dream that they're taking it again. It's equally common for people who have been tortured in prison to dream that they're back with their captors. Does that mean that they want to go back?

See the whole business of consuming alcohol for what it is: a horrible nightmare from which you have finally awoken for good.

YOUR FINAL DRINK

Perhaps it sounds contradictory to say alcohol does absolutely nothing for you, and then recommend you have a final drink. But if you don't mark the end of your drinking career with the milestone of a final drink, there's a danger you might sit around wondering whether or not you are truly free.

You're free once you've finished your final drink.

So let's not delay your escape a moment longer. Pour yourself a large measure of neat spirit, preferably the spirit you consider most foul. If there are no spirits in your home, use the strongest, most unpleasant alcoholic beverage you can find. Before you drink it, take time out to close your eyes and make a solemn vow that it will be your last ever alcoholic drink. As you drink it, concentrate on the vile taste, and reflect upon how you were once conned into paying a small fortune to pour this filthy poison down your throat. Then:

GET ON WITH ENJOYING YOUR LIFE!

Allen Carr Contact Information

Head Office 1c Amity Grove, London SW20 OLQ
Tel: +44 (0)20 8944 7761
Email: postmaster@allencarr.demon.co.uk
Web: www.allencarreasyway.com

Allen Carr's Easyway to Stop Drinking and **Easyweigh to Lose Weight** sessions are available at selected clinics only. Please contact your nearest Allen Carr's Easyway to Stop Smoking Clinic for latest details.

The following list gives details for **Allen Carr's Easyway to Stop Smoking Clinics** where we guarantee that you will stop smoking – or your money back.

UK
London Tel: 020 8944 7761
Website: www.allencarreasyway.com
Birmingham Tel: 0121 423 1227
Website: www.allencarreasyway.com
Brighton Tel: 0800 028 7257
Website: www.allencarreasyway.com
Buckinghamshire Tel: 0800 0197 017
Website: www.easywaybucks.co.uk

Bristol & Swindon Tel: 0117 950 1441
Website: www.easywaybristol.co.uk
Exeter Tel: 0117 950 1441
Website: www.easywayexeter.co.uk
Kent Tel: 01622 832 554
Website: ww.allencarrseasyway.com
Manchester Tel: 0800 804 6796
Website: www.easywaymanchester.co.uk
North East Tel: 0191 581 0449
Website: www.easywaynortheast.co.uk
Reading Tel: 0800 028 7257
Website: www.allencarrseasyway.com
Scotland Tel: 0845 450 1375
Website: www.easywayscotland.co.uk
Southampton Tel: 01425 272757
Website: www.allencarrseasyway.com
South Wales Tel: 0117 950 1441
Website: www.easywaycardiff.co.uk
Staines/Heathrow Tel: 0800 028 7257
Website: www.allencarrseasyway.com
Yorkshire Tel: 0800 804 6796
Website: www.easywaymanchester.co.uk

Worldwide Clinics

Check for your nearest clinics by visiting www.allencarrseasyway.com and clicking on "Clinic Locations" or visit the following websites:

Republic of Ireland www.easyway.ie
Australia www.allencarr.com.au
Austria www.allen-carr.at
Belgium www.allencarr.be or (French) www.allencarr.info
Canada www.allencarrseasyway.ca
Colombia www.esfacildejardefumar.com
Denmark www.easyway.dk
France www.allencarr.fr
Germany www.allen-carr.de
Italy www.easywayitalia.com
Mexico www.allencarr-mexico.com
Netherlands www.allencarr.nl
New Zealand www.easywaynz.co.nz or www.allencarr.co.nz
Norway www.easyway-norge.no
Portugal www.comodeixardefumar.com
South Africa www.allencarr.co.za
Spain www.comodejardefumar.com
Switzerland www.allen-carr.ch
UK www.allencarrseasyway.com
USA www.allencarrusa.com